Epilepsy

by Judith Peacock

Consultant:
John Thompson
Information and Referral Coordinator
Epilepsy Foundation of Minnesota

Perspectives on Disease and Illness

LifeMatters
an imprint of Capstone Press
Mankato, Minnesota

LifeMatters Books are published by Capstone Press
818 North Willow Street • Mankato, Minnesota 56001
http://www.capstone-press.com

Printed in the United States of America

Library of Congress Cataloging-in-Publication Data
Peacock, Judith, 1942–

      Epilepsy/by Judith Peacock; consultant, John Thompson.

         p. cm. — (Perspectives on disease and illness)

      Includes bibliographical references and index.

      Summary: Discusses types of epilepsy, causes, living with epilepsy, controlling seizures, current research, and more.

      ISBN 0-7368-0278-9 (book). — ISBN 0-7368-0294-0 (series)

      1. Epilepsy Juvenile literature. [1. Epilepsy. 2. Diseases.]

      I. Title. II. Series.

      RC372.P38 2000

      616.8´53—dc21   99-30562

                                   CIP

Staff Credits
Kristin Thoennes, editor; Adam Lazar, designer; Kimberly Danger, photo researcher

Photo Credits
Cover: PNI/©Digital Vision, bottom, left, right; PNI/©Rubberball, middle
Gerri Empy, 43
FPG International/©Telegraph Colour Library, 39
©Index Stock Photography, Inc./7, 15, 19, 24, 25, 33, 46
International Stock/©Richard Pharoh, 16; ©Michael Agliolo, 8; ©Tony Demin, 54; ©Jay Thomas, 59
Unicorn Stock Photos/©F. Pennington, 31; ©Jeff Greenberg, 49
Visuals Unlimited/©Jeff Greenberg, 11, 35, 50; ©Bill Beatty, 41; ©Rob Simpson, 56; ©SIU, 22

A 0 9 8 7 6 5 4 3 2 1

Table
of Contents

Chapter Overview

Epilepsy is the name for a variety of seizure disorders.

A seizure is sudden, abnormal activity in the brain. Brain cells misfire and cause an electrical overload. The person loses control of movement, thought, and/or awareness for a short time.

Many things can cause epileptic seizures. The exact cause of most seizures is unknown.

Epilepsy has been one of the most misunderstood disorders in history. Even today, people with epilepsy may be treated as outcasts.

Chapter 1

What Is Epilepsy?

Jack attends West High School. He is a smart guy, and he's funny. Jack likes sports, music, and cars.

Jack, Age 16

One day, Jack stood in line in the lunchroom. He began to see spots in front of his eyes. Suddenly he blacked out and fell to the floor. His arms and legs became stiff. Then his body jerked all over. Saliva appeared around his mouth. Jack wet his pants.

After a few minutes, Jack came to. He felt confused and tired. All he wanted to do was sleep.

Jack has epilepsy. He had a seizure in the lunchroom. Epilepsy is the name for a variety of seizure disorders.

In some cases, seizures involve only a very small part of the brain. The area may be no larger than the head of a pin.

A Seizure Disorder

Anybody can have a seizure, which can be epileptic or nonepileptic. Epileptic seizures result from a disorder of the brain and nervous system.

Nonepileptic seizures can occur for several reasons. The reasons include a sudden drop in blood pressure, low blood sugar, or stress. Withdrawal from alcohol or other drugs also can cause seizures.

An epileptic seizure is a sudden, temporary change in brain activity. Brain cells use electrical impulses to communicate with each other. They usually fire off messages in an orderly way. During a seizure, some cells go haywire. They fire off too many messages too fast. An epileptic seizure is like an electrical storm in the brain.

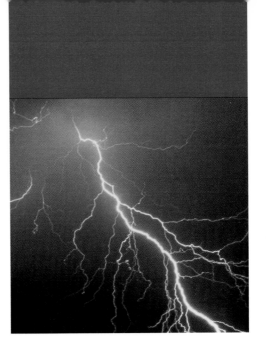

People with epilepsy lose control over movement, thought, awareness, or a combination of these. There are many forms of epilepsy. It might be a convulsion like the one Jack had. Convulsions are when the muscles contract in a violent and uncontrolled way. It might be a staring spell, temporary confusion, or a strange feeling. A seizure can be a minor bother, or it can be life threatening.

A person cannot stop a seizure after it starts. A seizure may last a few seconds or a few minutes. After a seizure, the brain cells are exhausted. It may take awhile before the person feels normal again.

Someone who has had only one seizure may not have epilepsy. People with epilepsy have had more than one seizure. The seizures have been at different times. The seizures occur again and again if not controlled.

What Causes Epilepsy?

Epilepsy is not a disease but can be caused by a disease. A high fever also can damage the brain.

Pete had meningitis when he was six years old. **Pete, Age 12** At first, everyone thought he had the flu. The doctor told Pete's mother to give him aspirin. Pete's fever became very high. He began to have seizures. The meningitis had infected the membrane that covers the brain. Pete's brain was scarred. There was no way to fix the damage. Pete's seizures continued after he became well.

Epilepsy has many other causes. They include the following:

Damage to a baby's brain before birth or after birth

A head injury

Poisons like lead or alcohol

A stroke or other disorder of the circulatory system

A brain tumor

Myth: A person having a seizure is going crazy.

Fact: People having seizures are not going crazy. They are the same people before and after the seizure.

Certain types of epilepsy are inherited. In addition, some people may inherit a tendency for seizures. These people are more likely than other people to have seizures.

Over one-half of the people with epilepsy never know the cause. Sometimes epilepsy develops right after an illness or injury. Other times epilepsy develops years after an illness or injury.

Who Gets Epilepsy?

In the United States, about 2.5 million people have epilepsy. In Canada, about 300,000 people have this disorder. Epilepsy affects all races. It can develop at any age, but 50 percent of cases develop before age 25. Males are slightly more likely than females to have epilepsy. Epilepsy is not contagious. It cannot be spread from person to person.

Epilepsy is usually a lifelong condition. Some children stop having seizures as they grow older. Some have new types as they grow older. Most people with epilepsy are likely to have seizures throughout life.

Many famous people in history have had epilepsy:

Alexander the Great
Julius Caesar
George Frideric Handel
Fyodor Dostoyevsky
Vincent van Gogh

Looking Back on Epilepsy

Epilepsy has been around since the beginning of time. Seizures both awed and frightened people. Many false ideas arose to explain seizures. The Greeks and Egyptians believed that people with epilepsy were prophets. Prophets are people who know and tell the future. It was thought that gods entered into a person during a seizure. People with epilepsy were considered gifted.

During the Middle Ages, church leaders believed that people with epilepsy were evil. Church leaders taught that demons caused a person to have seizures. People with epilepsy were treated as outcasts. They were tortured and murdered. Such myths continue in many parts of the world today.

North American history also contains many false ideas about epilepsy. People with epilepsy were thought to be insane or mentally retarded. They were locked up in hospitals and prisons. They were not allowed to go to school. Epilepsy was thought to be inherited in all cases. Laws prevented people with epilepsy from marrying or having children.

Scientists now know that epilepsy is a neurological disorder. This means that it is related to the nervous system. Scientists have found ways to treat seizures. Even so, many people today do not understand the disorder. They are afraid of people with epilepsy.

Rachel has had epilepsy since she was four **Rachel, Age 13** years old. She knows that kids in school can be mean. She has heard kids say, "Stay away from her! You'll get seizures." Sometimes Rachel wonders, "Which is worse? Having epilepsy or being made fun of?"

Points to Consider

Have you ever seen a person having a seizure? How did you feel? How did you react?

How would you feel if you saw a classmate having a seizure?

Do you know anyone who has epilepsy? How do others treat that person?

How much do you know about epilepsy?

Chapter Overview

There are two main types of epileptic seizures. Generalized seizures involve both sides of the brain. Partial seizures involve only a part of the brain.

Tonic clonic and absence seizures are generalized seizures. The person loses consciousness during these seizures.

The person does not lose consciousness during simple partial seizures. Consciousness, however, is usually somewhat impaired. The person cannot communicate normally during complex partial seizures.

Seizures usually do not harm a person. They do not change someone's personality. A person having a seizure is more likely to get hurt falling.

Chapter 2

Types of Epileptic Seizures

There are many different types of epileptic seizures. Most of them can be divided into two main groups. These groups are generalized seizures and partial seizures. Generalized seizures involve the whole brain. The person loses consciousness. Tonic clonic seizures and absence seizures are well-known generalized seizures.

Partial seizures involve just a part of the brain. The person's symptoms depend on the part of the brain affected. A partial seizure may spread to other parts of the brain. It may become a generalized seizure. Partial seizures can be simple or complex.

"I think I must look like a vampire when I have a seizure. I get blood in my mouth from biting my tongue."

—Tony, age 14

Tonic Clonic Seizures

Tonic clonic seizures are the most violent and frightening type of seizure. Most people think of this kind when they hear the word *epilepsy*. Only about 10 percent of seizures are strictly tonic clonic. Tonic clonic seizures used to be called grand mal seizures. Doctors no longer use this term.

A tonic clonic seizure may begin with a loud cry. Air is escaping from the person's lungs. During the tonic stage, the body stiffens and falls to the ground.

During the clonic stage, the body jerks around. The tongue rolls back in the mouth. The person cannot swallow. This may cause saliva to build up on the lips. The person's breathing slows and may even stop. The skin turns blue-gray. The person may lose bladder control.

A tonic clonic seizure lasts only a few minutes. Normal breathing returns. Consciousness also returns, but the person may feel tired and confused. He or she does not remember what happened before or during the seizure. It may take awhile before the person is fully aware.

Absence Seizures

Heidi sat in English class. She had a blank look on her face. Her eyelids moved up and down rapidly.

Heidi, Age 12

"Heidi, do you know the answer?" asked Miss Foster.

"What?" said Heidi. "I didn't hear the question."

"You need to pay better attention, Heidi. What are the subject and verb in this sentence?"

Heidi seemed to be daydreaming. She was actually having an absence seizure. Absence seizures used to be called petit mal seizures. Doctors no longer use this term.

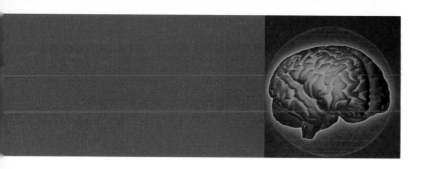

During an absence seizure, the person appears to be staring into space. The eyelids and face muscles may twitch. The mouth may make chewing movements. Absence seizures last only a few seconds. Afterward, the person goes back to what he or she was doing. A person can have more than 50 absence seizures in one day.

Absence seizures are most common in children. Parents, teachers, and other adults may not notice them. They may think the child just has difficulty paying attention.

Other Types of Generalized Seizures

There are other common types of generalized seizures. During a myoclonic seizure, the whole body or a part of the body jerks suddenly. The person may fall out of a chair or drop something. He or she seems clumsy.

During an atonic seizure, the person's body suddenly goes limp. He or she collapses and falls. The person becomes fully aware after a few seconds and can stand and walk. This type of seizure is also called a drop attack. Someone having an atonic seizure may appear drunk.

Infantile spasms appear in babies and toddlers. Spasms are quick, sudden movements. It may be hard to tell the difference between spasms and normal baby movements.

Myth: You can tell a person has epilepsy by looking at him or her.

Fact: People with epilepsy look like anyone else. The only way you could tell is if you saw the person having a noticeable seizure.

Simple Partial Seizures

A simple partial seizure can affect movement, emotions, and the senses. Uncontrolled jerking can occur in any part of the body. The person may suddenly feel fear, anger, sadness, or joy. The person may hear sounds or see sights that are not really there. He or she may experience odd tastes and smells. The person remains conscious during this type of seizure. He or she knows what is happening and usually can talk to other people.

Complex Partial Seizures

Jim, Age 17

"Jim, where's your math homework?" asked Mr. Lang.

Jim didn't answer. He appeared to be in a daze. For several minutes, he kept grabbing his nose. "My nose is bugging me. My nose is bugging me," Jim said over and over. Finally he stopped.

The other kids laughed. "He's at it again," someone said.

Some people with epilepsy have a strange sensation before a seizure. It might be a feeling or a certain taste or smell. This is called an aura. The aura is actually a simple partial seizure. A person's aura is always the same. The aura warns the person that a seizure is coming.

Jim has complex partial seizures. This type of seizure involves more of the brain than simple partial seizures. The person is conscious, but consciousness is impaired. The individual cannot communicate in a normal way with other people.

Complex partial seizures usually begin with a blank stare. The person mumbles and repeats certain actions. The actions are the same from seizure to seizure. He or she may pick up objects, walk in circles, run, or take off clothing. When the seizure is over, the person does not remember what happened. People with complex partial seizures may seem mentally ill or drunk. This is the most common type of seizure among adults.

Are Seizures Dangerous?

Tonic clonic seizures that last longer than a few minutes may injure the brain. Nonstop seizures may result in death due to lack of oxygen. Most seizures end naturally, however, and do not harm the brain.

The place in which a seizure occurs can be more dangerous than the seizure itself. People with generalized seizures might break a bone if they fall on a hard floor or down steps. They might cut themselves on nearby sharp objects. People with complex partial seizures might wander into a busy street. A person who has a seizure while swimming could drown. Seizures sometimes occur during sleep. Then there is the risk of suffocation.

People with epilepsy cannot deliberately harm others during a seizure. They are not in control of their body or mind.

Points to Consider

Why is it important to know what different types of seizures are like?

How should a teacher handle a student's seizure at school?

A classmate thinks it's funny to pretend to have a seizure. What would you say or do?

Chapter Overview

Diagnosing epilepsy can be difficult. There are many different types of epileptic seizures. A seizure might indicate a condition other than epilepsy.

Doctors use the results of a physical examination and medical tests to diagnose epilepsy. They also consider the person's medical history and age. A description of the person's seizures helps determine the type of seizure.

There are tests that measure the activity of the brain and that show the structure of the brain.

A diagnosis of epilepsy can be very upsetting. Counselors can help people accept the diagnosis.

Chapter 3

Diagnosing Epilepsy

Doctors are careful in diagnosing epilepsy. They want to know if a person's seizures are epileptic or have another cause. If possible, they want to find out the type of epileptic seizure. An accurate diagnosis helps doctors plan the most effective treatment.

Symptoms of Epilepsy

One evening Amy sat at the dinner table with her family. Suddenly, her hand began jerking. Her fork flew out of her hand. A few minutes later, the fork went flying again. The family thought Amy was clumsy or nervous.

Amy, Age 13

In the next few weeks, Amy's right hand continued jerking. The jerking spread to her right arm. Other strange things began happening. Amy felt like throwing up all the time. Her face muscles twitched. She smelled rotten eggs when no one else did. Amy's parents decided to take Amy to the doctor.

A convulsion is the most obvious sign of epilepsy. Amy did not have a convulsion, but she did have other symptoms. She could not keep her hand and arm from jerking. She had an upset stomach, or nausea. She had hallucinations. This is when people see, hear, or taste things that aren't really there. Symptoms of epilepsy also might include the following:

Periods of confusion or fear
Blackouts
Staring spells
Being unaware of surroundings
Difficulty following directions
Sudden strange tastes, sights, or sounds
Repeated actions or movements

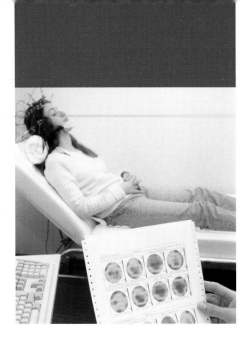

Amy's family doctor suggested that Amy see a neurologist. A neurologist is a doctor who specializes in problems of the nervous system.

Amy Goes to the Doctor

The neurologist began the diagnosis by noting Amy's symptoms. He asked about her medical history. He wanted to know about past illnesses and injuries. The doctor looked into Amy's eyes. He observed how she reacted to stimulants and observed her movements.

An eyewitness description of a seizure is a valuable part of diagnosis. The doctor asked Amy's parents to describe her seizures. He wanted to know when they happened and how long they lasted. He also wanted to know what she did during the seizures.

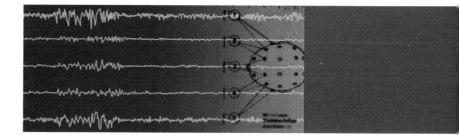

Medical Tests

The main test for epilepsy is an electroencephalogram, or EEG. An EEG measures brain activity. It may show abnormal brain activity.

Amy Is Tested for Epilepsy

Amy went to the hospital for her EEG. The nurse pasted small metal disks on Amy's scalp. The disks were electrodes. A wire was attached to each electrode. At the other end, the wires were connected to a machine. The machine monitored the pattern of electrical activity in Amy's brain. It printed the results onto sheets of paper.

The electrodes were attached for 24 hours. The doctor wanted to test her asleep and awake. A video camera recorded her movements. Amy saw herself in a mirror and laughed. The wires sticking out of her head looked like something from outer space.

Myth: An EEG test can read a person's mind.

Fact: An EEG only measures brain signals. It cannot read a person's mind.

An EEG may not always show signs of epilepsy for two reasons. First, the seizure may take place deep in the brain. The wires on the scalp cannot sense the seizure. Second, the person may not have a seizure during the EEG.

A doctor may order other tests besides an EEG. A CAT scan and an MRI use computer technology. They provide pictures of the brain. The doctor can check the pictures for scar tissue and for tumors. The person must lie very still for these tests.

After the Diagnosis

Diagnosing epilepsy can be complicated because of the many different types of seizures. Different types of seizures may look similar. A person may have more than one type of seizure. In Amy's case, the doctor diagnosed simple partial seizures. He prescribed a drug for this type of seizure. If the drug does not work, Amy will come back for more tests.

Yolanda is a pro when it comes to epilepsy. She has these practical tips for newly diagnosed teens:

- Think of a way to help you remember to take your pills. I use a pillbox. I bought it for 99 cents at the drugstore.

  - Keep a journal of your seizures. It will help your doctor know more about your type of seizure.

    - Always sing in the shower. That way your family will know you're all right.

Amy's Diagnosis

Amy and her parents were shocked at the doctor's diagnosis. They could not believe that Amy had epilepsy. They felt angry and sad. The doctor said that Amy would be fine. He gave them the telephone number of a local epilepsy organization. People there help families learn more about epilepsy. They also help people like Amy and her family deal with their feelings about epilepsy.

Points to Consider

Have you had an EEG, a CAT scan, or an MRI? Has anyone in your family had these medical tests? What was the reason? What was the outcome?

What would you do if you found out you had epilepsy?

How would you cope if someone in your family had epilepsy?

Chapter Overview

Epilepsy cannot be cured. Treatment for epilepsy consists of controlling seizures. Antiseizure drugs are the most common way to control seizures.

Brain surgery may help people for whom drugs are not effective. There are several types of surgery.

A high-fat, or ketogenic, diet may help some children control their seizures.

People with epilepsy should try to avoid things that trigger their seizures.

It is important for people to work together with their doctor on a treatment plan.

Chapter 4

Controlling Seizures

The treatment for epilepsy has one goal—to control seizures.
There is no cure for epilepsy at the present time.

Antiseizure Drugs

Antiseizure drugs are the most common way to control seizures.
These drugs prevent or reduce the number of seizures. They help
most people with epilepsy take control of their seizures.

Many different drugs are available to treat epilepsy. It is tricky to
find the right drug for a person. Doctors must consider the type of
epilepsy. They also must consider the person's sex, weight, age,
and reactions to medicine. If possible, doctors try to control
seizures with just one medicine. Sometimes, though, two or three
drugs are necessary.

**Common side effects
from antiseizure medication include:**

- Drowsiness
- Lack of energy
- Crankiness
- Difficulty in walking
- Difficulties with memory
  and thinking
- Personality change

- Upset stomach
- Gum overgrowth
- Slurred speech
- Blurred vision
- Hair loss or gain
- Weight loss or gain

Finding the correct medicine may take several months to a year or longer. During this time, the person should keep track of how well a drug controls the seizures.

The doctor periodically tests the person's blood for the level of medicine in it. Too much medicine may cause sleepiness, difficulty walking, mood changes, and other troublesome side effects. Too little medicine may not help in preventing seizures. The doctor tries to find the right dosage.

The Right Dosage at the Right Time

People with epilepsy need to take their medicine regularly. A steady supply of medicine needs to be in the blood. It is not a good idea to skip doses or take fewer pills. This is true even if no seizures have occurred for a long time. Skipping or taking too few doses may make the drug level too low to control seizures.

A person's medicine may need to be adjusted from time to time. This is especially true as children grow older. Sometimes children are given larger doses of medicine than adults are. It takes more medicine to control a child's seizures. During the teen years, the child's body becomes more like that of an adult. If teens continue the same dosage, they may become overmedicated.

People with epilepsy usually must take antiseizure drugs for the rest of their life. Sometimes people think they can stop taking their medicine. They might think this if they have not had a seizure for a long time. People with epilepsy should always talk with a doctor before going off their drugs. It can be dangerous to quit too abruptly.

Tonic clonic and absence seizures were diagnosed in Will when he was nine years old. By the time he got to high school, Will was tired of taking pills. He hated the way they made him feel. None of his friends took medicine. Will wanted to be normal.

Will, Age 15

Will started flushing his pills down the toilet. He didn't tell his mother. For a while, things were all right. Then Will began having seizures almost every day. He had several seizures in school. He certainly didn't feel normal then.

Will's mother took him to a new doctor. Will liked this doctor. He was able to talk with her. The doctor helped Will understand how the drugs controlled his seizures. Together they found a drug that didn't make Will feel sick. Will didn't mind taking his pills so much after that.

The brain feels no pain. That is why a person can be awake during brain surgery. Painkillers numb the feeling in the layers of bone and skin protecting the brain.

Surgery

Antiseizure drugs do not help about 20 percent of people with epilepsy. Brain surgery may be an option for these people. Doctors must be able to operate without damaging other parts of the brain. The surgery should not take away the person's ability to see, hear, think, and remember. Surgery is always a risk, however.

Skilled surgeons perform surgery for epilepsy. It is usually done at special epilepsy centers rather than in local hospitals. Before surgery, the person must go through several tests.

The person may be awake during all or part of the operation. The surgeon uses a tiny electric probe to locate different areas of the brain. The person answers questions to help the surgeon locate where problems occur. This is called brain mapping. After surgery, the person may need to take antiseizure drugs for a year or two.

Types of Surgery

Several types of surgery are performed for epilepsy. One type takes out a small amount of brain tissue. This surgery is performed when seizures start in just one part of the brain. A second type cuts nerve fibers that connect one side of the brain to the other. This surgery is performed when seizures affect both sides of the brain. Cutting nerve fibers may prevent the spread of a seizure. A third type removes all or almost all of one side of the brain. This operation is performed in children who have severe seizures.

Eric, Age 16

Eric had surgery for epilepsy when he was five. At the time, he had almost nonstop seizures. He had to stay in the house and wear a helmet to protect his head. Antiseizure drugs only left him in a fog. The doctors said he might die without surgery.

Eric doesn't remember the operation. He does remember the green gelatin and fun bed in the hospital. Eric is glad he had the surgery. It left him with partial vision in his right eye, but he doesn't mind. He has been almost seizure-free since the surgery. It's great to be able to do things other kids do.

A small percentage of people with epilepsy are sensitive to light. Sunshine or flickering lights can trigger seizures in those individuals. Teens have had seizures while watching TV or playing video games.

Ketogenic Diet

A ketogenic diet may prevent seizures in young children. This special diet is high in fats such as butter, cream, eggs, and red meat. When the body burns all that fat, it produces molecules called ketones. For some unknown reason, the ketones seem to stop seizures.

A food specialist called a dietitian must work out a ketogenic diet. The diet must be carefully followed, just like a drug treatment. Food must be weighed and measured. Studies are under way to see if a ketogenic diet can help teens with seizures.

Seizure Triggers

Another way to control seizures is to avoid seizure triggers. Seizure triggers are things that can set off a seizure. They do not cause seizures, but they increase the chances that a seizure will occur.

Seizure triggers vary from person to person. Julie, for example, is more likely to have seizures in hot weather. Levi's seizures seem to come when he drinks too much soda pop. Kate has more seizures around the time of her period. Lack of sleep, poor eating habits, and stress trigger seizures in many people with epilepsy. For these reasons, it is important to practice good health habits.

Alcohol and street drugs harm people in many ways. They can cause seizures in people who do not have epilepsy. They are especially dangerous for people who already have a seizure disorder. It is never a good idea to mix alcohol and street drugs with antiseizure drugs.

Crystal, Age 18

Crystal is a high school senior with epilepsy. Every Friday night, she went out with her girlfriends. They usually drank a lot of alcohol. Crystal came home, threw up, and went to bed. Every Saturday Crystal had a seizure. She finally realized that the alcohol triggered the seizures.

Crystal decided to stop drinking. Her friends stopped calling her. She was very depressed. After a few weeks, Crystal began to make new friends. These friends did not pressure her to drink. Things started looking up again.

Points to Consider

What might be some advantages and disadvantages of each treatment for epilepsy?

Why might treating epilepsy be expensive?

Why might it be hard for a teen with epilepsy to follow a treatment plan?

How could you help a friend with epilepsy stick to his or her treatment plan?

Chapter Overview

First aid begins by recognizing the seizure type. Tonic clonic seizures and complex partial seizures may require first aid. First aid usually is not needed for absence seizures and simple partial seizures.

First aid for seizures consists mainly of keeping the person safe. Epileptic seizures usually end on their own in a few minutes. It is important to remain calm and help others remain calm.

It is important to know when to call an ambulance for a seizure. Onlookers often call an ambulance unnecessarily.

Risk of injury during a seizure can be reduced.

Chapter 5

Safety and Appropriate Response to Seizures

Seizures can occur any time and any place. It is important to know first aid for seizures. Doing the wrong thing can harm the person having a seizure. It is also important to prepare for seizures. This helps reduce the risk of injury and even death.

Myth: When a person has a seizure, put a pencil, spoon, ruler, or other hard object in the mouth. This will keep the person from swallowing his or her tongue.

Fact: **NEVER** put anything in the mouth of a person having a seizure. This may cause the person to choke or cause other mouth or dental injury.

First Aid for Tonic Clonic Seizures

Max, Age 16

Max and his friend Ginger stood in line to buy tickets to the movie. They heard a cry and then a thud. The woman in line behind them was on the floor. Her body jerked from side to side. The other people in the lobby gasped and stared.

"What's wrong with her?" asked one man. He stepped back nervously.

"I think she's having a heart attack," said another.

"No, it's a seizure," a woman shrieked. "Quick! Put a pencil or something in her mouth!"

"Call 911!" someone in the crowd yelled.

A seizure can be a frightening thing to watch. People who do not know about seizures can panic. They may do the wrong things. Fortunately, Max saw that the woman was having a tonic clonic seizure. He had learned first aid for seizures in his health class. Max was able to help the woman.

This is what Max learned to do for a tonic clonic seizure:

Stay calm.

Look for medical identification.

Time the seizure. If it lasts longer than five minutes, call an ambulance.

Clear the area of dangerous objects.

Loosen the person's necktie, shirt collar, or scarf.

Protect the head from injury. Put something soft and flat under the head.

Turn the person on his or her side to prevent choking. Do not turn the person if there is an injury.

Comfort the person as consciousness returns.

This is what Max learned NOT to do for a tonic clonic seizure:

Do not put anything in the person's mouth.

Do not try to hold the tongue.

Do not give liquids during or just after the seizure.

Do not give artificial respiration unless the person has inhaled water or is not breathing after muscle jerks stop.

Do not try to restrain or hold the person down.

The Epilepsy Foundation of America suggests turning a person having a seizure onto his or her side. This may help keep the airway clear.

First Aid for Complex Partial Seizures

Becky, Age 17

Becky waited for the bus from downtown to home. She heard a lot of car horns honking. Becky looked toward the street. A man was standing in the middle of rush-hour traffic. "What in the world?" Becky wondered. "Is that guy drunk?"

Becky watched as a police officer gently guided the man toward the curb. The officer spoke calmly to the man. The officer had him sit down on the bench where Becky was sitting. After a few minutes, the man seemed to come to. The officer offered the man a ride home in her squad car.

The police officer did all the right things. She recognized that the man was having a complex partial seizure. A person having this type of seizure seems to be in a trance or sleepwalking. It is important not to use force against the person. He or she may fight back uncontrollably.

This is what the police officer knew to do for a complex partial seizure:

Speak calmly to the person.

Guide the person gently away from danger.

Stay with the person until he or she is fully aware.

Offer help getting home.

This is what the police officer knew NOT to do:

Do not grab the person unless he or she is in immediate danger.

Do not try to hold the person back.

Do not shout.

Do not expect the person to obey spoken orders.

Do not call an ambulance immediately.

When to Call an Ambulance

When people see someone having a seizure, they may call an ambulance immediately. This may be the wrong thing to do. Most often, a tonic clonic seizure will end after a few minutes. The person will come out of it naturally. He or she may feel tired and confused but will be all right. Taking the person to the hospital runs up needless medical bills for that person. The bills for the ambulance and emergency room could total hundreds of dollars.

On the other hand, there are times when an ambulance should be called.

An ambulance should be called if the person:

Has seizures that do not stop after five minutes

Has one seizure after another

Is pregnant

Injures himself or herself

Has diabetes

Has never had a seizure before

Has a seizure that takes place in water

Many people with epilepsy say their dogs warn them of upcoming seizures. The dogs warn their owners by barking, licking their owner's face, or staring. Some dogs make sure nothing covers their owner's mouth during a seizure. The dogs may even turn people on their side. Researchers are studying the claims of dog owners.

Safety and Seizures

People with epilepsy can prepare for their safety during a seizure. This is especially important if seizures are frequent and severe. People with epilepsy might do the following:

Make sure family and friends know first aid for seizures. First aid for choking is also helpful.

Wear a medical identification bracelet or necklace, or carry a medical ID card. A medical ID helps strangers know what to do.

Safety-proof the house. This will reduce the risk of bruises, breaks, and cuts in a fall.

Avoid handling dangerous objects or doing dangerous tasks when alone. A seizure at these times could result in extreme injury or even death.

Use appliances and motor-driven equipment that have automatic shut-off switches.

Plan participation in sports activities carefully and think about the potential for injury, especially in high-risk situations.

Points to Consider

Have you learned first aid for seizures? If not, what could you do to make sure you have this knowledge?

How can you help a person who is recovering from a seizure?

Why might police mistakenly arrest a person having a complex partial seizure?

What areas of your school might be hazardous for a person having a seizure? What could you do to make your school safer for a person with epilepsy?

Chapter Overview

The teen years can be a difficult time for any young person. Teens with epilepsy face even more challenges.

Teens with epilepsy may have difficulty with schoolwork. Their families may be afraid to let them do things. Dating and driving present special problems. Fear of seizures may lower teens' confidence and self-esteem.

There are ways to cope with the challenges of epilepsy. Teens can take charge of their epilepsy.

Chapter 6

Living With Epilepsy

Most teens with epilepsy lead a normal life. They go to school, make friends, get jobs, and have fun. Even so, living with epilepsy can present challenges. Teens with hard-to-control seizures may have an especially difficult time.

Fears

Teens with epilepsy may live in fear of having a seizure. They do not know when the next seizure will happen. They may worry about having a seizure in front of classmates. Fear of having seizures may keep teens from going places and doing things.

Family

Epilepsy affects the family, too. The whole family can be on edge. Everyone wonders when the next seizure will happen. The family may need to change plans at the last minute because a child had a seizure. Parents usually must give extra attention to a child with epilepsy. Other children in the family may feel jealous. They may feel embarrassed about their sibling's seizures.

Families often overprotect a child with epilepsy. They may want to keep the child at home. This causes problems for teens with epilepsy who want to be on their own.

School

Teens with epilepsy may have more difficulty with schoolwork. The type of seizure may affect memory and concentration. A teen with absence seizures, for example, may miss directions and other information. The side effects of antiseizure drugs may cause teens to feel sleepy all the time. Teens with epilepsy may have a hard time staying awake in class. They also may have difficulty finishing exams and assignments on time.

You can find out about laws regarding driving and seizures from your local department of motor vehicles.

Brett misses a lot of school because of his seizures. After a seizure, he is tired and confused. He needs up to two hours to recover. Brett's old school used to send him home every time he had a seizure. In his new school, he spends this time sleeping in the nurse's office. Brett forgets everything he learned right before the seizure. He must learn it all over again.

Brett, Age 13

Driving

Teens everywhere look forward to getting their driver's license. Getting a license may be a problem for teens with epilepsy. All states have laws about losing consciousness while driving. A person must be seizure-free for a certain length of time before he or she can get a license. The waiting period may vary from three months to one year. If a teen has a seizure during that time, he or she must start the waiting period over.

Not being able to get a driver's license can be hard. Teens may feel left out if they are unable to drive. Other teens may wonder what is wrong.

Young men with epilepsy must register for the Selective Service even though they cannot serve in combat positions.

Dating

Dating is another important concern for teens. Teens with epilepsy may have special concerns. They wonder if anyone will want to go out with them. Should they tell their dates about their epilepsy? What if they have a seizure while on a date? What if they have a seizure while kissing?

> Nan got all dressed up to go on her first date with Tom. She looked terrific. Sure enough, the thing she feared most happened. Her arm started jerking and shaking. It happened four times during the evening. Tom didn't say anything, but the two never went out again.
>
> **Nan, Age 16**

Planning a Career

Many teens begin making plans for a job or career after high school. People with epilepsy can do almost any kind of work. There are a few exceptions, though. People with epilepsy cannot be an airline pilot or a bus driver. They cannot serve in a combat position in the military. A seizure while performing these jobs might endanger the lives of others.

Teens with epilepsy need to think about their seizure triggers when deciding on a career. Some careers involve a high level of stress and long hours. Stress and fatigue are two common seizure triggers.

Coping With Epilepsy

Teens who face the challenge of their epilepsy have a better life. They learn many skills in dealing with their seizures. They can apply these skills to other areas of their life. If you are a teen with epilepsy, here are ways to cope:

Work to overcome fear of seizures.

Talk about your feelings with your doctor, family, or friends. Join a support group for teens with epilepsy. Do things to reduce the chance of a seizure. For example, follow your treatment plan and avoid seizure triggers. Find out everything you can about seizures. Knowing about epilepsy will help you feel in control.

Start in small ways to become independent.

While still living at home, learn to do more things for yourself. Be responsible for your own medication. Watch out for your own health and safety. Do chores around the house. Learn to cook and to handle money.

Find out your rights as a student.
By law, public schools must provide an education that fits your needs. If necessary, ask your teachers to make a few changes for you. For example, ask for more time to take tests. Tape-record lectures and class discussions. If you miss something, you can listen to the tape. If you are behind in school, ask for a tutor.

Accept the fact that you may be unable to drive.
Public transportation can take you many places you want to go. Friends and family can provide rides, too. Most people with epilepsy eventually get their license.

Don't blame your epilepsy for everything.
A boyfriend or girlfriend may choose to break up with you. Your seizures may or may not be the cause. Something else may be the reason. Sometimes people just don't have as much in common as they thought.

Get involved in an organization that helps people with epilepsy.
Organizations such as the Epilepsy Foundation of America provide many services to people with epilepsy. These include information about epilepsy, counseling, employment assistance, and recreational activities. These organizations also provide support groups and workshops for families.

Teens with epilepsy may have emotional problems. Epilepsy itself does not cause feelings of worthlessness and despair. Rather, these problems result from other people's attitudes toward epilepsy.

Points to Consider

Do you know anyone who lives with a chronic illness? How does that person cope?

Your friends at school refuse to acknowledge a student with epilepsy. What would you do?

Do you think doctors should have to report patients with epilepsy to the driver's license department? Why or why not?

Chapter Overview

Ongoing research on the brain may lead to a cure for epilepsy.

Researchers are developing better ways to control seizures.
One of the most promising new treatments is vagus
nerve stimulation.

Laws guaranteeing legal rights help to improve the life of
people with epilepsy.

The public needs to know the facts about epilepsy. Too many
false ideas still exist. Teens with epilepsy, their family, and
their friends can help in the fight against epilepsy.

Chapter 7

Looking Ahead

The future for people with epilepsy looks bright. Much is being done to improve the diagnosis and treatment of epilepsy. The fight for legal rights for people with epilepsy continues. More is being done to educate the public about epilepsy.

Finding a Cure

Research is under way to find a cure for epilepsy. Scientists are studying the brain to find out more about seizures. They want to know the answers to many questions: Why do seizures begin? Why are some people more likely to have seizures than others? Why do seizures sometimes start years after a blow to the head? What role does heredity play in seizures?

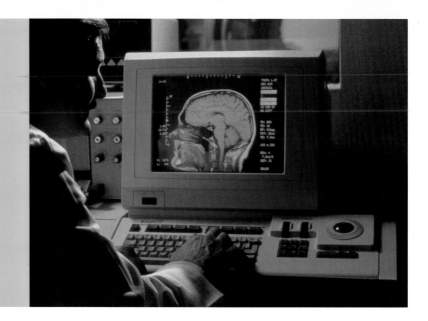

Developing Better Ways to Treat Seizures

Scientists and doctors are developing better ways to treat seizures.
These include the following:

New drugs to control specific types of seizures and drugs
with few side effects.

New equipment and procedures to make surgery safe and
effective. Laser surgery can be performed without cutting
open the skull. This surgery also can go deeper into the brain.

New technology that pinpoints the location of a person's
seizures. Surgeons will know exactly what part of the brain
to remove. This will make surgery possible for more people.

Myth: People with epilepsy are mentally retarded.

Fact: People with epilepsy have the same range of intelligence as the general population.

Another new and exciting treatment for seizures is called vagus nerve stimulation (VNS).

Josh, Age 15

Josh is 15 years old. He has had frequent and uncontrolled seizures for most of his life. He could not ride a bike, swim, or cross the street. In junior high, his teachers had to walk him from class to class. He felt like a baby.

A few months ago, surgeons implanted a small electrode in Josh's chest. Wires run under his skin from the electrode to the vagus nerve. The vagus nerve carries information to the brain. Josh's doctor programmed the electrode to fit Josh's pattern of seizures. The electrode automatically sends mild shocks to Josh's brain. The stimulation interrupts and stops seizures.

Josh also can use a special magnet to stop seizures. If he feels a seizure coming on, he holds the magnet close to the electrode. The magnet activates the electrode. Josh's parents can use the magnet as well.

Josh has been almost seizure-free since he started VNS therapy. He can do many more things. Best of all, he can go from class to class by himself.

Fighting for Legal Rights

Not too many years ago, people with epilepsy were denied basic rights. Things have improved, but there is still work to do. Laws now protect people with epilepsy from discrimination in employment.

People with epilepsy also have the right to enjoy public places. They can use public transportation. Organizations such as the Epilepsy Foundation of America seek to uphold these rights. They also work for new laws that will help people with epilepsy. For example, people with epilepsy sometimes have difficulty getting affordable life, health, or auto insurance. New laws could change this situation.

Educating the Public

Many people still have negative attitudes about epilepsy. They may not want to be around people with epilepsy. They may not want to give people with epilepsy a fair chance at work, school, or play. People with epilepsy, their family, and their friends need to help change public opinion.

Karen's little brother, Joey, has epilepsy.  **Karen, Age 18** People stare at Joey when he has seizures. This makes Karen mad. She also gets mad when other children won't play with him.

Karen thinks people should know more about epilepsy. Maybe then they wouldn't be so cruel. Karen has explained epilepsy to her friends. She gave a report on epilepsy in her health class. She passed out leaflets about epilepsy during Epilepsy Awareness Month. Karen likes to have people ask questions about Joey. This gives her a chance to tell the facts about epilepsy.

As recently as 1982, some states had laws forbidding people with epilepsy from marrying.

Preventing Epilepsy

Another important part of public education is telling people how to prevent epilepsy. Protecting the brain from damage can sometimes prevent epilepsy.

Pregnant women can help avoid brain damage in their unborn babies. They can eat a healthy diet and not use alcohol and other drugs. They also can stay away from situations in which they risk injury.

After birth, infants should always be strapped into infant seats when in a car. Parents should have their children immunized against measles and other diseases. Children should never be shaken or hit, and especially not in the face or head.

Everyone should follow rules for safety and good health. This includes driving safely and wearing seat belts. People should wear helmets when bicycling, skating, skateboarding, or riding a motorcycle. Prescription drugs should be taken only as directed.

Points to Consider

What are some ways you could help raise money for epilepsy research and treatment?

What can you do to educate other people about epilepsy?

What can your school do to educate students and teachers about epilepsy?

Do you wear a helmet when you ride your bike or skateboard? Do you wear a seat belt when you're in a car? Why or why not?

Glossary

chronic (KRON-ik)—lasting for a long time; a person with a chronic disease or disorder may have it throughout life.

consciousness (KON-shuhss-nuhss)—state of being aware

contagious (kuhn-TAY-juhss)—capable of being spread from person to person

convulsion (kuhn-VUHL-shuhn)—a series of violent and uncontrolled contractions of the muscles

diabetes (dye-uh-BEE-teez)—a condition in which the body does not use blood glucose properly; too much sugar builds up in the blood.

epilepsy (EP-uh-lep-see)—a disorder of the brain and nervous system

generalized seizure (JEN-ruh-lyezd SEE-zhuhr)—one of the main types of epileptic seizures

hallucination (huh-loo-suhn-AY-shuhn)—seeing, hearing, or tasting things that are not really there

immunize (IM-yuh-nize)—to make someone able to resist a disease

meningitis (men-in-JYE-tiss)—an inflammation of the membranes that surround the brain and spinal cord

nausea (NAW-zee-uh)—upset stomach

neurological (nur-uh-LAH-ji-kuhl)—relating to the nerves and nervous system

neurologist (noo-RAHL-uh-jist)—a doctor who specializes in disorders of the nervous system

partial seizure (PAR-shuhl SEE-zhuhr)—one of the main types of epileptic seizures

seizure (SEE-zhuhr)—sudden, abnormal activity in the brain

For More Information

Aaseng, Nathan, and Jay Aaseng. *Head Injuries*. New York: Franklin Watts, 1996.

Dudley, Mark E., and Susan S. Spencer. *Health Watch: Epilepsy*. Parsippany, NJ: Crestwood House, 1996.

Huegel, Kelly. *Young People and Chronic Illness*. Minneapolis: Free Spirit, 1998.

Landau, Elaine. *Epilepsy*. New York: Twenty-First Century Books, 1995.

Schachter, Steven C., Georgia D. Montouris, and John M. Pellock. *The Brainstorms Family: Epilepsy on Our Terms*. Philadelphia: Lippincott-Raven, 1996.

Useful Addresses and Internet Sites

Epilepsy Foundation of America
4351 Garden City Drive
Landover, MD 20785
1-800-EFA-1000

Epilepsy Ontario National Office
1 Promenade Circle, Suite 308
Thornhill, ON L4J 4P8
CANADA
1-800-463-1119 (in Canada)

National Institute of Neurological Disorders
and Strokes
National Institutes of Health
Department of Health and Human Services
Building 31, Rooms 8A-16
Bethesda, MD 20892

National Information Center for Children and
Youth With Disabilities
PO Box 1492
Washington, DC 20013
1-800-695-0285

Epilepsy Foundation of America
http://www.efa.org
Offers information on epilepsy; has a teen
chat room

Teenagers With Epilepsy
http://www.geocities.com/HotSprings/spa/1453/
index.html
A resource dedicated to teens with epilepsy;
provides links to other sites

Epilepsy
http://www.gillettechildrens.org/epilepsy.html
Provides general information on epilepsy

Internet Resources for Special Children
http://www.irsc.org
Provides information to and promotes public
awareness of children with disabilities

Index